MEDIEVAL MEDICINE

Nicola Barber

Raintree

www.raintreepublishers.co.uk
Visit our website to find out
more information about
Raintree books.

To order:
☎ Phone 0845 6044371
🖷 Fax +44 (0) 1865 312263
🖳 Email myorders@raintreepublishers.co.uk

Customers from outside the UK please telephone +44 1865 312262

Raintree is an imprint of Capstone Global Library
Limited, a company incorporated in England and
Wales having its registered office at 7 Pilgrim Street,
London, EC4V 6LB – Registered company number:
6695582

Edited by Andrew Farrow, Adam Miller, and
  Vaarunika Dharmapala
Designed by Philippa Jenkins
Original illustrations © Capstone Global Library
  Ltd 2013
Illustrations by International Mapping
Picture research by Ruth Blair
Originated by Capstone Global Library Ltd
Printed and bound in China by Leo Paper
  Products Ltd

ISBN 978 1 406 23871 6 (hardback)
16 15 14 13 12
10 9 8 7 6 5 4 3 2 1

British Library Cataloguing in Publication Data
Barber, Nicola.
Medieval medicine. -- (Medicine through the ages)
610.9'02-dc22
A full catalogue record for this book is available
from the British Library.

Acknowledgements
We would like to thank the following for permission
to reproduce photographs: Bridgeman Art Library
pp. 26 (Islamic School, [14th century]/Biblioteca
Estense, Modena, Italy), 31 (Italian School/Biblioteca
Universitaria, Bologna, Italy/Archives Charmet);
Corbis pp. 5 (© Massimo Listri), 37 (© Bettmann);
© Corbis p. 21; Getty Images pp. 4 (Fratelli Alinari/
Alinari Archives), 9, 22 (Hulton Archive), 19 (Marvin
Lichtner/Time Life Pictures), 18 (India Today
Group), 27 (Alinari Archives), 33 (The Bridgeman
Art Library/French School), 34 (Mansell/Time Life
Pictures); Mary Evans Picture Library pp. 12, 17
(Interfoto/Sammlung Rauch), 24; Science Photo
Library pp. 16 (NYPL), 32 (Sheila Terry); The Art
Archive pp. 8 (Episcopal Museum Vic Catalonia/
Gianni Dagli Orti), 28 (University Library Istanbul/
Gianni Dagli Orti); Wellcome Library, London pp. 6,
7, 10, 11, 14, 15, 23, 25, 29, 30, 35, 36, 38, 39, 40, 41.

Cover photograph of *Cutting out the Stone of Madness
or an Operation on the Head* by Pieter Bruegel the
Elder (c.1525–1569), reproduced with permission of
Bridgeman Art Library (Musée de l'Hotel Sandelin,
Saint-Omer, France/Giraudon).

Every effort has been made to contact copyright
holders of any material reproduced in this book.
Any omissions will be rectified in subsequent
printings if notice is given to the publisher.

Contents

Some words are shown in bold, **like this**. You can find out what they mean by looking in the glossary. You can also look out for them in the "Word Station" box at the bottom of each page.

A backwards step?

The time in European history known as the medieval period, or the Middle Ages, started around AD 500 and lasted until roughly 1400. It began when the empire created by the Romans, which had dominated much of Europe for around four centuries, finally disintegrated. In AD 410, Rome was attacked and looted by a Germanic tribe called the Visigoths, the first time the city had been occupied by foreign invaders for nearly 800 years.

By AD 500, the western half of the Roman Empire had been overrun and settled by the Visigoths, Ostrogoths, Vandals, and other tribes to create a patchwork of kingdoms with ever-changing borders.

This is the remains of an aqueduct bridge built by the ancient Romans to supply the city of Rome with fresh water. By the third century AD, there were 11 such aqueducts carrying water into the city.

Health and medicine in ancient Rome

The fragmentation (break-up) of the Roman Empire had implications for both medical practice and learning in Europe. The Romans had understood the link between cleanliness and general health and, as a result, they were pioneers of **public health** projects.

In Rome, for example, **aqueducts** were built to bring fresh water into the city and sewage systems to take waste out. Personal hygiene was encouraged by the construction of large public bath houses, which charged a small fee. All over their empire, the Romans built similar services for their towns and cities.

The Romans relied on their armies to control and defend their vast empire, so they also understood the importance of keeping their soldiers fit and healthy. Forts were often equipped with baths, **latrines**, and aqueducts. Some also had hospitals (*valetudinaria*) to care for sick or injured Roman soldiers. The remains of these early hospitals have been uncovered at Roman forts in many parts of Europe. In this way, Roman medical knowledge and practices were spread widely during the time of the empire.

This early painting shows dentists at work on a patient.

The movements of peoples and frequent wars that marked the end of the Roman Empire disrupted life for many communities across Europe. The public health systems set up by the Romans were either destroyed by war or fell into disuse and disrepair. Travel became more difficult and dangerous, affecting both trade and communications.

In many places, libraries containing medical manuscripts were destroyed and education was disrupted. Rulers who were often at war with each other were more interested in defending their states and kingdoms than in encouraging learning and scholarship.

WORD STATION
public health prevention of disease and promotion of health through the organization of a community

5

Medieval medicine

Much medical knowledge was lost at the end of the Roman Empire. The increasingly powerful Christian Church also played an important part in medical belief. Christianity was the religion of the Roman Empire from the fourth century AD, and in the following centuries much of Europe became Christian.

During the early Middle Ages, Christian **monasteries** were the main centres of learning and scholarship. It was in monastery libraries that the surviving Greek and Roman medical manuscripts were preserved, read, translated, and copied by monks. These manuscripts included a few texts by the ancient Greek **physician** Hippocrates, and by two Greek physicians who practised during the time of the Roman Empire, Dioscorides and Galen.

DIOSCORIDES
(C. AD 40–90)

Dioscorides was a physician and **pharmacologist**. He travelled widely around the Roman Empire in his role as a surgeon to the armies of Emperor Nero. He wrote *De Materia Medica* ("About Medical Materials"), a five-volume encyclopedia about plants, herbs, and other substances used in medicines. This work provided the basis for many of the texts about medicinal herbs ("herbals") written in the early Middle Ages.

Did you know?
In *De Materia Medica* Dioscorides describes nearly 600 plants. In fact, his book remained the basic source of knowledge about medicinal plants for around 1,500 years.

This page from an Arabic translation of Dioscorides' *De Matria Medica* shows medicine being prepared from a wild vine.

WORD STATION
pharmacologist someone who specializes in the preparation and study of drugs

Vol. V.   G. P. Busch Sculp.

GALENVS

Galen was famous in his own lifetime both as a physician and as a philosopher. He wrote many texts on a wide variety of subjects.

GALEN
(AD 129–C.216)

Galen studied and travelled widely, and became an extremely successful physician. He carried out **dissections** on animals to improve his surgical skills and to learn about **anatomy**. He demonstrated that **arteries** carry blood (not air as believed previously). Galen's theories about how the body works shaped medical thinking for the next 1,400 years.

As a young physician, Galen worked in a gladiator school in Pergamum (in modern-day Turkey), where he learned a great deal about treating wounds. He later moved to Rome where he was a physician to several emperors.

However, it was in the Islamic world of the Middle East that the main developments in medicine took place during the medieval period (see pages 26–29), including many translations of ancient Greek and Roman texts into Arabic. From the late 11th century onwards, more of Galen's works were translated into Latin. It was Galen's theories that formed the basis of medical education in the new medieval universities (see pages 30–33).

The Christian Church

The beliefs of the Christian Church had a huge influence on the development of medicine in the medieval period. In the early Middle Ages, the Church taught that everything, including disease, came from God and formed part of God's greater plan. Illness was often considered to be a divine punishment for sins and as such the proper remedy was prayer and **repentance**. Any attempt to treat or heal an illness was seen as interfering with God's will.

Over time, the Church's attitude towards illness altered. The work of caring for the sick and the poor became an important part of Christian charity. The human body was seen as the creation of God, and therefore to be looked after. The practice of medicine, for example preparing herbal cures, became an accepted part of Christian teaching.

This painting from the 14th century shows a woman kneeling before a priest for an exorcism (a ritual to drive out an evil spirit).

WORD STATION
repentance act of repenting a sin – that is, admitting wrong and trying to do better

This casket, dating from the 13th century, depicts the death and burial of Archbishop Thomas Becket. It would have once held relics of his life.

THOMAS BECKET'S SHRINE

In 1170, Archbishop Thomas Becket was murdered by four of King Henry II's knights as he knelt at the altar in Canterbury Cathedral. Immediately after his death, rumours of miracles began to spread. It was said that several local women were cured of their sickness after touching one of the cloths used to wipe Becket's blood off the cathedral floor.

Over the following years, thousands of pilgrims flocked to Becket's shrine in Canterbury, in the hope of miraculous cures. In 1173, only three years after his death, Becket was made a saint.

Shrines and relics

Alongside these beliefs, people also turned to the accounts of miracle cures in the New Testament of the Bible. The various healing miracles of Jesus, for example restoring the sight of a blind man, encouraged strong popular belief in the supernatural. In particular, people turned to the healing powers of certain saints (holy people), and places associated with these saints, known as shrines. Many of these shrines housed relics – fragments such as bones, teeth, or clothes, or personal objects – that were said to come from important Christian saints. People made pilgrimages from far and wide to worship at these shrines, and to pray for cures for their ailments.

Centres of healing

The Christian Church provided the earliest centres of healing in medieval Europe. Many clerics had some medical knowledge, passed down from the ancient texts that survived mainly in cathedral and **monastery** libraries (see page 6). Monasteries and **convents** set up infirmaries where monks and nuns were cared for when they were ill. Monasteries also began to build public hospices. These were places for pilgrims to stay, and for the poor and needy, but they also provided some care for the sick. The term *hospital* (from hospitality) was therefore originally far more general than its modern meaning.

This illustration from a 17th-century manuscript shows a monk giving three men medicine for their eye injuries. His room is filled with many jars of medicine.

The central role of the Church in medieval medicine meant that it was quite usual for a sick person to consult both a priest and a **physician** or healer in the search for a cure. Some churchmen became famous for their medical learning and for their powers of healing. John of Beverley, born in Yorkshire, was renowned in his lifetime for the miracles he performed, particularly for giving a mute boy the ability to talk. He was made a saint after his death in AD 721.

WORD STATION
monastery religious community run by monks

Patron saints of medicine

- St Luke is the **patron saint** of physicians. He was himself a physician, and probably accompanied St Paul on his journeys around the Middle East.

- St Cosmas and St Damian were twin brothers who both studied medicine. They became well known for treating people without demanding payment, and converting many to Christianity as a result. They were tortured and put to death during a time of Roman persecutions, in around AD 300, for refusing to give up their Christian beliefs. They are the patron saints of **pharmacy** and medicine. The painting on the right shows the brothers performing a miraculous leg transplant, attended by angels.

- St Apollonia also suffered for her faith at the hands of the Romans. It is claimed that she was tortured by having her teeth extracted before being burned to death in AD 249. As a result, she became the patron saint of tooth problems, and sufferers of toothache in medieval times were often advised to offer up prayers to her.

Beliefs and practices

Besides religious beliefs, there were other theories about illness during the medieval period. The basis of these ideas was the theory of the four **humours**, which was passed down from the ancient Greeks. This theory was central to the teachings of Hippocrates and Galen, and it remained an important influence in European medicine all the way through to the 1800s.

The "humours" were four liquids – blood, **phlegm**, black **bile**, and yellow bile – believed to be present in the human body. According to this theory, people became ill when the balance between the humours was disturbed. As a result, medieval treatments for illness were usually concerned with trying to restore the correct balance of humours in the body.

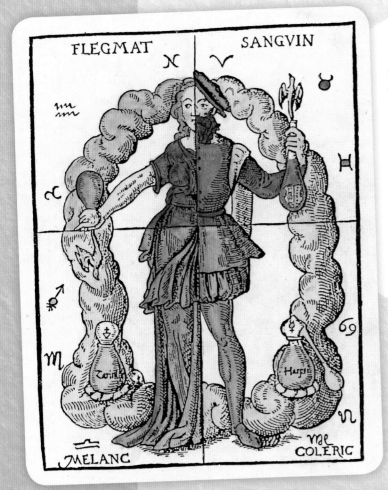

Different personality types were represented by each of the four humours. Phlegm was associated with an individual being phlegmatic (unemotional), blood with being sanguine (optimistic), black bile with being melancholic (sad), and yellow bile with being choleric (irritable).

WORD STATION
bile in medieval medical theory, two of the four humours are black and yellow bile. Bile is a bitter liquid produced by the liver, which helps the digestion of food.

A universal theory

In medieval belief, the theory of the four humours was a universal theory – the four liquids inside the body were linked with elements in the outside world. So the four humours were each associated with air, water, earth, and fire; the four seasons; certain qualities (hot, cold, wet, dry); and the four ages of mankind (childhood, youth, adulthood, old age). Doctors believed, for example, that in winter the body was prone to having too much phlegm (the humour associated with winter).

Keeping a balance

Doctors in parts of the world beyond medieval Europe had theories about the importance of balance within the body that had similarities to the four humours. In China, people believed in an energy force, known as *chi*, that runs through the body. This energy has two opposite forces, *yin* and *yang*, which need to be kept in balance for a healthy body.

In India, the time between the fifth and eighth century AD was when the main texts of Ayurveda were written. The Ayurvedic system emphasized staying healthy by keeping three energies (the three *doshas*) in balance in the body. Like European **physicians**, Chinese and Indian doctors used herbs to prepare treatments for sick patients. You can find out more about Chinese and Indian medicine in *Ancient Medicine*, another book in this series.

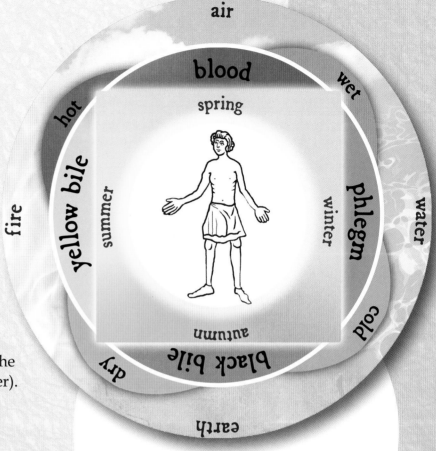

The four humours were linked with elements from nature. You can see here that yellow bile, for example, was associated with summer and fire.

Diet and exercise

In his writings, Galen recommended a range of treatments for illness, including massage, exercise, and changes to diet. Medieval doctors used Galen's ideas, often in combination with herbal remedies and **bloodletting** (cutting open a vein to allow blood to flow out). Most people's diet was made up of grains such as wheat and oats, with a little meat or fish when available. Vegetables and fruit were eaten when they were in season. If harvests were poor, then people went hungry and their health suffered.

Medieval diet also changed according to the season. This meant food was often scarce in winter. Lack of vitamin C, which is found in fresh fruit and vegetables, caused a disease called **scurvy**, which made people's gums soft and spongy and loosened their teeth. Evidence from archaeological finds at a medieval hospital in Scotland suggest that monks there used watercress (which we now know is a good source of vitamin C) to combat the effects of scurvy. Although they did not understand the reasons why their teeth were falling out, the monks knew that something in the watercress helped to prevent this problem.

 This illustration from the 16th century shows herbs and plants being prepared for use as medicines.

WORD STATION
scurvy disease caused by lack of vitamin C

Wort-cunning

Wort-cunning was the knowledge of herbs and their preparation (in this case, *wort* means herb and *cunning* means skill). Medieval remedies were made from every part of a plant. Some remedies used the sap or resin from trees to make drinks or, mixed with animal fat, lotions. Most remedies were made from herbs and plants that grew locally, but some needed herbs that came from other countries. Sugar was believed to be particularly effective for many afflictions, including bladder problems.

This is a page from a leech-book compiled in the 16th century.

The use of herbs in
medieval medicine was
based on the belief that
all natural treatments
were God-given, and
that God had marked
many natural objects
with a "signature"
as an indication of
their usefulness. This
theory later became
known as the doctrine
of signatures. For
example, toothwort with
its tooth-like flowers
was used to treat
problems with teeth.

"Simples"

Medieval healers and physicians used a wide range of plants to treat
ailments. Modern-day medical historians who have studied medieval
remedies have found that many of these treatments were effective to
some degree. These are a few examples of healing herbs, often known
as "simples":

- Camomile was taken for headaches and stomach complaints.
- Garlic was used to prevent or treat almost every ailment.
- Mint was very common in foods and medicines. It was used to help
  digestion and for bad breath.
- Myrrh, a dried tree resin, was used as an antiseptic on wounds and
  to treat bleeding gums.
- St John's wort was used to treat burns.
- Vervaine (verbena) was so widely used for so many ailments that it
  was given the name "simpler's joy".

This page comes
from a copy of
Dioscorides' *De Materia
Medica* (see page 6)
made in the 16th century.
It illustrates some
commonly used medicinal
plants, including foxglove
and cowslip.

This medieval illustration shows a patient undergoing bloodletting.

THE KING'S TOUCH

In medieval England and France, kings and queens were believed to have special God-given healing powers. It was thought that the royal touch could cure a skin disease called scrofula. The symptoms of this disease – swellings in the neck – were actually caused by tuberculosis. This practice began in the 11th century during the reigns of Edward the Confessor in England and Philip I in France.

Bloodletting

Medieval physicians believed that another way to restore balance within the body of a sick person was to make a cut and allow blood to flow out. Bloodletting was believed to release excess humours. Cuts were made in various parts of the body depending on the ailment being treated. Sometimes blood-sucking leeches were put on to the skin to remove blood, or to clean out an infected wound. Bloodletting was usually carried out by a barber-surgeon or surgeon (see page 33). Today we know the dangers of losing large amounts of blood, and many patients must have died as a result of this treatment.

Public health and plague

In the early centuries of the Middle Ages, towns and cities were generally filthy and **unsanitary** places. They did not have systems of sewers and water pipes seen in Roman settlements, and there was no proper disposal of rubbish and **excrement**. Many medieval towns grew quickly in size as a result of increased trade. York, for example, expanded rapidly in the 9th and 10th centuries as Viking invaders and traders settled in the city. The narrow streets were covered in a layer of rubbish made up partly of rotting food and animal dung. In fact, so much rubbish filled the streets that the level of the town rose by about one centimetre every year.

THE GREAT CONDUIT

In 1236, work started on the first organized water supply to the medieval city of London. The City obtained the rights to a spring of fresh water outside its boundaries at Tyburn. Over the following 30 years, a lead pipeline, known as the "great conduit", was constructed to carry the water into London so that "the rich and middling persons therein might have water for preparing their food, and the poor for their drink".

Organized water supplies were built all over the world during the medieval period. This huge well with steps is now a World Heritage Site in India.

WORD STATION
unsanitary dirty and unhygienic

These wooden combs were found at a Viking settlement in Greenland. Viking combs found at Jorvik in northern England were made from antler or bone.

Personal hygiene

Toilets in Viking York were outdoor cesspits – holes dug in the ground and covered with earth – which often polluted local water sources. People suffered from worms and stomach upsets from drinking and cooking food in dirty water, as well as more serious diseases such as **dysentery** and **cholera**.

However, people did make an effort to keep themselves personally clean, and there was an understanding of the link between cleanliness and good health. Large numbers of combs have been found in excavations of Viking York, probably used by the inhabitants to comb head lice and fleas out of their hair.

COMMON CONFUSIONS

Cold wash

It is so easy for us to shower or take a bath that it is hard to remember how difficult it was for people in medieval times to keep clean. Only the wealthiest households could afford to heat water to fill a wooden tub for bathing. For ordinary people, the only way to wash was in cold water in the nearest stream or river, or with a bowl of cold water.

Spreading disease

The Middle Ages was a time of movements of peoples across Europe. The Vikings left their homes in Scandinavia to conquer and settle lands in countries such as Britain and Iceland, while the Normans invaded Britain in 1066. As people moved to new lands, they took their germs and diseases with them.

In 1334, there was an outbreak of a deadly and infectious disease, known as the plague, in China. Over the next few years, the disease travelled westwards, carried by merchants along the trade routes from China, and by Mongol tribes. In 1346, it reached Caffa, a trading centre on the Black Sea, which was under the control of Italian merchants. The Mongols laid siege to Caffa and, according to some stories, catapulted plague-infected bodies into the city. The Italians took to their ships and fled – but it was too late. By 1350, the plague had spread across most of Europe, killing millions as it went.

This map shows the spread of the plague – known as the Black Death – across Europe between 1347 and 1350.

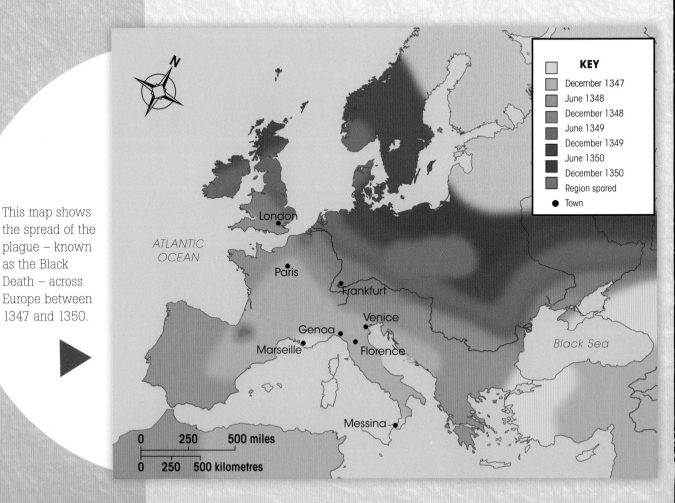

KEY
December 1347
June 1348
December 1348
June 1349
December 1349
June 1350
December 1350
Region spared
● Town

ATLANTIC OCEAN

London
Paris
Frankfurt
Venice
Genoa
Marseille
Florence
Messina
Black Sea

N

0   250   500 miles
0   250   500 kilometres

This image from a 15th-century manuscript shows two victims of the Black Death. You can clearly see the swellings ("buboes") on their bodies.

Three types of plague

The most common form of plague was bubonic plague, named after **buboes**, the swellings that appeared in a victim's armpits, neck, and groin area. Symptoms included headaches, vomiting, and high fever. Without any effective medical treatment, around two-thirds of sufferers eventually died.

The second type, pneumonic plague, infected the lungs. Victims coughed up blood and mucus, and most died very quickly. This type of plague was particularly dangerous because it was spread by bacteria in the air, which meant that a person could breathe it in. The least common form, septicaemic plague, may have been the origin of the grisly name "Black Death". The bacteria infected the victim's bloodstream, often turning the skin black. This type of plague usually killed in a matter of hours.

What was the plague?

No one in the 14th century knew what the plague was or how it was passed on. Many people believed that it was a punishment from God for human wickedness. Modern science has argued that the plague was spread by a **microbe** called *Yersinia pestis*. This microbe lives in the bloodstream of rats, and it also infects the fleas that live on the rats. Rat fleas also bite humans, and so pass on the microbe. However, scientists are still debating the causes of the plague. Today, some believe it was passed from person to person, and not by rats after all.

Cito, Longe, Tarde

It is difficult to imagine the terror that must have gripped medieval communities when the plague hit. The quotations from the Italian writers Marchione di Coppo Stefani and Giovanni Boccaccio give us an insight into the horrific conditions endured by both victims and survivors of the Black Death in Florence. **Physicians** could offer little help except to follow Galen's advice: "Leave quickly, go far away, and come back slowly" (in Latin, *Cito, Longe, Tarde*). People fled from towns and cities into the countryside to avoid infection, but often only succeeded in spreading it even further.

Plague remedies

While some people simply waited for death, others tried a variety of remedies. Many people believed that the plague spread through "bad air", so they burned incense to try to cleanse the air around them. Doctors advised people to cover their doors and windows with heavy cloths to keep poisonous air out of their houses. Many people covered their faces with scented cloths whenever they went out. It was also believed that sound might drive the plague away – some communities rang church bells or even fired cannons.

As this medieval illustration shows, one of the measures taken to prevent the spread of the Black Death was the burning of clothes believed to be infected with the disease.

Procession des Disciplinans.

The people shown in this etching are whipping themselves. They hoped that God would take away the plague if they showed repentance for their sins.

> "Many died daily or nightly in the public streets; of many others, who died at home, the departure was hardly observed by their neighbours, until the stench of their putrefying [rotting] bodies carried the tidings; and what with their corpses and the corpses of others who died on every hand the whole place was a sepulcher [tomb or grave]."

Giovanni Boccaccio
The Decameron

> "Neither physicians nor medicines were effective. Whether because these illnesses were previously unknown or because physicians had not previously studied them, there seemed to be no cure. There was such a fear that no one seemed to know what to do. When it took hold in a house it often happened that no one remained who had not died."

Marchione di Coppo Stefani
Florentine Chronicle

EXTREME MEASURES

Groups of flagellants believed that only public acts of **repentance** would soothe the angry God who had sent the plague. They travelled from place to place, whipping themselves until they bled. Other people, looking for someone to blame for the catastrophe, turned on minority groups such as the Jews, gypsies, or lepers (see pages 24–25).

Public health measures

Some towns and cities, particularly in Italy, took measures to try to control the spread of plague. In 1348, Venice closed its waters to ships suspected of carrying the disease and enforced a period of **quarantine** before crews were allowed to land. Other Italian cities restricted people's movements. Many places also established hospitals, called "pesthouses", where victims of plague were isolated from the rest of the community. Despite this, thousands of people died in Italy. It is estimated that by the end of the 14th century, the Black Death had wiped out between 20 and 30 million people, around one-third of the entire population of Europe.

This medieval illustration shows a man on crutches entering a leper hospital. During the 12th century, thousands of such hospitals were built across Europe. By 1225, it is thought there were around 19,000.

Leprosy

Another disease that was widespread during the Middle Ages, and which caused great suffering, was leprosy. Leprosy attacks a person's skin and nerves, and often results in the victim's nose, toes, or fingers becoming deformed. It is a very visible disease, and in medieval times it was believed to be extremely infectious.

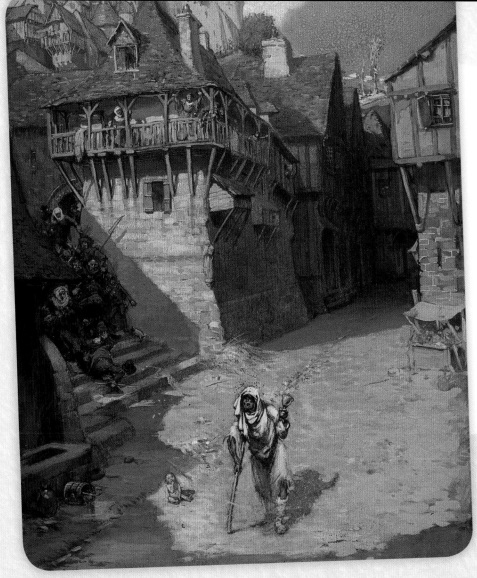

This painting from a later period shows how people would scramble to get away from a leper. In order to warn of his approach, the leper rings a bell as he walks.

RAVEN'S EGG TEST

Deciding if someone had leprosy was a tricky business, and it was often carried out by a priest. One odd method involved placing a raven's egg into a bowl of the suspect's blood. If the egg hardened, the person was believed to have leprosy!

Today, leprosy is completely curable, but in the Middle Ages there was no cure and it was so feared that people suffering from the disease were excluded from society. In England, victims were forced to wear distinctive clothing and carry bells or clappers to warn people of their approach. Lepers, as they were known, were not permitted to go into churches or inns, or drink from public fountains. They were, however, allowed to beg, and in many medieval towns some food was set aside to provide for them.

In many places, lepers were excluded by forcing them to live in leper hospitals or communities, called *leprosaria* or lazar houses. This meant leaving their families for good. Leprosy was often referred to as the "living death", because sufferers were treated by those they left behind as though they were already dead.

Islamic medicine

While medieval Europe was experiencing the aftermath of the end of the Roman Empire, a new empire was being created across the Middle East, north Africa, and Asia. This empire was based on the new religion of Islam that began in Arabia early in the seventh century AD. By the mid-eighth century, followers of Islam, known as Muslims, had taken control of a vast area that extended from Spain in the west to Afghanistan in the east. The capital of this empire was Baghdad, which became a major centre for science and the arts.

In Baghdad, and elsewhere in the Islamic Empire, **physicians** collected and studied the works of the ancient Greek and Roman writers, including Hippocrates, Dioscorides, and Galen. They translated these texts into Arabic, as well as writing their own works about medicine. Muslim, Christian, and Jewish physicians, speaking many different languages, all contributed to medical knowledge of the time.

This manuscript from the 14th century shows a page from the *Canon of Medicine* by Ibn Sina (see page 28). Ibn Sina, also known as Avicenna, was an Islamic scholar who wrote widely about many topics including medicine. He lived from 980 to 1037.

Islamic scholars

Hunayn ibn Ishaq (AD 808–873), also known as Johannitius, was a Christian who studied medicine in Baghdad and became chief physician at the court of the Caliph (Islamic ruler). He travelled around the Islamic empire to collect ancient Greek manuscripts, and translated them into Arabic. He is famous for his many translations of Galen, which became the basis for medical knowledge in the Islamic Empire and, from the late 11th century onwards, in Europe.

Tacuinum Sanitatis

Tacuinum Sanitatis was a handbook of health based on a medical manuscript by Ibn Butlan, a Christian physician who lived and worked in Baghdad in the 11th century. Ibn Butlan's work was made up of 40 charts which identified the medical properties and uses of 210 plants and animals. It also suggested that exercise, sleep, and the balance of the **humours** were essential for good health. Ibn Butlan's manuscript was translated into Latin in the 13th century. It became extremely popular in the late Middle Ages, with some lavishly illustrated versions. It must be remembered, however, that most ordinary people did not have access to books, and most could not read – there was nothing like the general level of medical and health awareness that we take for granted today.

This picture is from the *Tacuinum Sanitatis*. It shows a shopkeeper selling camphor, a chemical used for medical purposes.

Alchemy and medicine

To a modern reader, it may seem odd that alchemy and medicine were once so closely linked. Many scholars and physicians were fascinated by the search for a method of turning cheap "base" metals such as lead or copper into silver or gold. Al-Razi, in particular, was a famous alchemist who wrote many texts about his findings.

No one ever succeeded in transforming base metals into rare ones. However, the practical processes of extracting, refining, and mixing liquids that were developed by the alchemists did become important in the preparation of medicines.

The influence of Al-Razi and Ibn Sina

Al-Razi (c. AD 854–925/935), also known as Rhazes, was born in Persia (modern-day Iran). He was a great scholar but also a practical physician. He was the first person to identify the differences between measles and smallpox. He wrote many works, including two medical encyclopedias that summed up Greek and Arabic medical knowledge of the time. They became standard texts for Islamic and European doctors for many centuries. He also wrote the first general medical advice book, which he dedicated to the poor, to travellers, and to those who could not afford a doctor.

This illustration from a 17th-century manuscript shows the physician Ibn Sina preparing a smallpox remedy.

Abdullah ibn-Sina (c. AD 980–1037), or Avicenna, was one of the most celebrated physicians and philosophers of the Islamic world. He wrote many texts, including *The Canon of Medicine*, which became an important textbook for medical scholars until the late 18th century. He incorporated ideas from all parts of the Islamic Empire into his work, including theories from the Ayurvedic system (see page 13).

Medicines

Physicians in the Islamic world based their knowledge of herbs, as well as animal products and minerals, on the Greek tradition. However, the Islamic Empire covered such a wide area that many previously unknown items were added to the list, such as camphor (a type of waxy gum from trees in Asia), senna (an African shrub), and nutmeg (a spice from Indonesia).

By the ninth century AD, the preparation of medicines had become a separate profession, carried out by **apothecaries** who often had their own shops. Some medicines were made from single herbs, but others required great expertise and the mixing of up to 100 different ingredients.

Earthenware jars similar to this one were used to store medicines in apothecary shops.

Doctors, surgeons, and hospitals

Medieval doctors **diagnosed** illnesses using the theory of the four **humours** (see page 12). They looked at the colour of the patient's skin, and often examined a patient's urine and blood to try to work out the cause of an illness. Doctors frequently checked the positions of the planets and the Moon before deciding on treatment, as they were believed to have an effect on bodily humours. However, only a small number of wealthy people visited the doctor. The majority of the population could not afford a doctor. When people fell ill, they were mostly cared for by family members, usually women, who often had some skill and knowledge with herbs and remedies. People also consulted local healers and wise women (see page 39).

Urine charts, such as this one from the 16th century, were used by medieval physicians. They believed the colour of the urine indicated certain illnesses.

WORD STATION
diagnose identify the nature of a disease or injury through examination

By the 11th century, doctors from all over Europe were travelling to the medical school at Salerno, in Italy to study medicine.

Medical training

In the early Middle Ages, doctors were not formally trained – most learned their skills by watching other, more experienced doctors at work. From the 11th century onwards, however, larger urban populations with more wealth created an increasing demand for **physicians** and a new interest in medical learning. The first medical schools were established in the 10th century in Italy.

During the 12th and 13th centuries, new universities were founded in cities such as Bologna in Italy, and Paris in France. While both men and women had studied at the first medical school in Salerno, Italy, women were not allowed to attend university. By the 13th century, anyone who wanted to become a doctor had to study and gain qualifications at university.

CHAUCER'S DOCTOR

Geoffrey Chaucer (1342/3–1400) is best-known for *The Canterbury Tales,* a collection of stories told by a group of pilgrims on their way to Canterbury. One of the pilgrims is a doctor, and Chaucer makes it clear that he knew not only about "physic" (medicine), surgery, and the four humours, but also astronomy:

"With us there was
A Doctor of Physic;
In all this world was
there none him like,
To speak of physic
and of surgery,
For he was
grounded in
astronomy
…
He knew the cause
of every malady,
Were it of hot,
or cold, or moist,
or dry,
And where they
engendered
[developed], and of
what humour.
He was a very
perfect practitioner."

University training

Training to become a doctor at university took a long time and students were normally the sons of noblemen or wealthy townspeople who could afford the costs of many years of study. Students studied for a general arts degree before specializing in medicine. Medical students studied the texts of Galen, Hippocrates, and Dioscorides, as well as Al-Razi and Ibn Sina. Many of these texts had been translated from Arabic into Latin in the 11th century by a monk known as Constantine the African who worked in the **monastery** of Monte Cassino, close to the medical school at Salerno.

Dissection and surgery

From the early 14th century, medical schools taught students about human **anatomy** by **dissecting** a corpse. Dissection had not been allowed by the Catholic Church during the early Middle Ages. The first public dissection, which took place around 1315 in Bologna, Italy, used the body of an executed criminal. The practice of using criminals' bodies became acceptable to the Church authorities, provided the body was given a proper Christian burial afterwards.

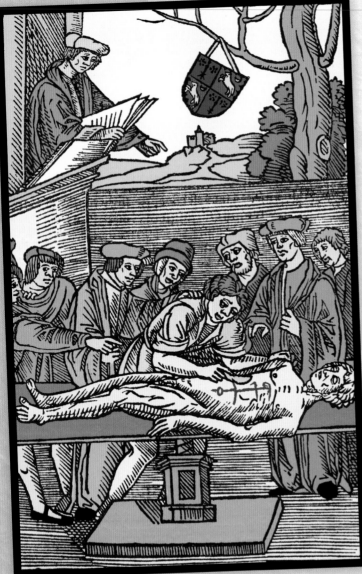

This artwork shows the first public dissection, performed at the University of Bologna, Italy in around 1315. The task of cutting the body was left to an assistant while the physician directed proceedings from above, and students looked on.

WORD STATION
anatomy bodily structure of a human, animal, or plant

Although medieval physicians learned all about the workings of the human body, they did not undertake treatment that involved cutting the body. This was the job of surgeons, and from the 13th century training for physicians and surgeons was separated. This separation probably originated in the fact that most medical work was undertaken by clerics in the early Middle Ages, including **bloodletting**. In 1163, however, the Church forbade monks to shed blood. Responsibility for surgery passed to barbers, who were experienced with razors (see page 35). Surgery was considered to be of a lower status compared to the work of physicians. It was not generally taught in universities, and most surgeons learned their craft as apprentices.

This is a page from Abn al-Qasim al-Zahrawi's encyclopedia. In the middle, you can see illustrations of a variety of surgical instruments.

ABU AL-QASIM AL-ZAHRAWI
(C. AD 936–1013)

Abu al-Qasim, also known as Albucasis, was born in Cordoba, which was then part of Muslim Spain. He was a renowned surgeon who wrote a 30-volume medical encyclopedia that was used for centuries afterwards in European and Islamic medicine. The encyclopedia includes sections on eye diseases, **cauterization**, treatment of fractures and dislocations, and childbirth (including the use of forceps).

Did you know?
In his encyclopedia, al-Qasim included a section that described and illustrated nearly 200 surgical instruments, many of which he designed himself.

صورة طبيب وشكلات وصورة عليل بو نكردذر

This illustration shows a doctor cauterizing his patient's wound with a hot iron.

Common procedures

Some of the most common **procedures** performed by medieval surgeons included fixing broken bones, bloodletting, cupping, and cauterizing wounds. Cupping was an alternative to bleeding to release excess humours from the body. A cup was heated and placed on the skin so that it drew blood to the surface. This technique had been used in ancient Greece and was common in the Islamic world. Cauterizing was a technique to treat wounds by applying boiling oil or hot irons. Cauterization was believed to prevent infection. It was also used to treat internal problems, and textbooks showed surgeons where to apply the cauterizing irons for different ailments.

Medieval surgeons also performed operations such as fixing **hernias**, or removing kidney stones. Such surgery was usually a last resort, as patients often died from shock, blood loss, or infection from dirty instruments. Although medieval doctors used wine to clean out wounds, there was no understanding of the direct link between dirt and infection. There is plenty of evidence from medieval manuscripts that attempts were made to **anaesthetize** patients during surgery. A variety of strong and dangerous drugs, including opium, mandrake, and hemlock, were used to make an anaesthetic potion called *dwale*. A cloth or sponge soaked in *dwale* was placed over the patient's mouth and nose. However, *dwale* was probably not as effective as a modern anaesthetic, and its effects could, at times, be lethal.

This patient is having his tooth pulled out by a barber-surgeon. The instrument used is similar to a pair of pliers.

Hospitals

The earliest hospitals in Europe were run by monks and nuns in monasteries and **convents**. From the 12th century, as Europe became wealthier, more hospitals were founded in towns and cities, often paid for by local government or wealthy patrons. One of the largest of these hospitals was Santa Maria Nuova in Florence, Italy, founded in 1288. It started with 12 beds, but by 1376 it had 62 beds for men and 58 for women, in separate dormitories. This expansion went hand-in-hand with a change of emphasis from caring for the "sick *and* poor" to the "sick poor". Wealthier people were usually treated at home.

BARBER-SURGEONS

Barber-surgeons shaved and cut hair to provide their daily income, and they also performed surgery. Some barber-surgeons learned their trade as apprentices to more experienced surgeons, but many were untrained and often illiterate. They frequently carried out work such as bloodletting, extracting teeth, or treating boils, as well as treating those injured in battles.

Not for everyone

In England, one of the biggest medieval hospitals was St Leonard's in York, founded early in the 12th century. By the 13th century, it had over 200 beds for the sick and poor. Not everyone was welcome at the new hospitals. Many refused to admit pregnant women, people who were considered insane, lepers, and anyone who was considered to be infectious. Hospitals refused pregnant women because they were not seen as "ill", so could not be attended by men.

In the late Middle Ages, some hospitals began to be associated with certain illnesses or certain groups of people, for example the Bethlem Royal Hospital ("Bedlam") in London looked after people with mental illnesses.

Islamic hospitals

Large hospitals were being built in the Islamic world from the ninth century AD. These hospitals were places of treatment and education. They had wards, a **pharmacy**, lecture rooms and a library for study, and a retirement home for the elderly poor. Physicians made regular ward rounds to assess patients, taking their students with them to teach as they went. The famous

physician Al-Razi acknowledged in his writings how much he learned by treating patients at the hospital in Baghdad. The painting on the left shows Abu al-Qasim al-Zahrawi treating a patient at a hospital in Cordoba, Spain.

This drawing shows the inside of the Hôtel-Dieu hospital in Paris. You can see that patients shared beds.

The life of a medieval hospital

The everyday work of caring for the sick in European medieval hospitals was carried out by monks and nuns. When an ill person first came to a hospital, it was usual for a cleric to ritually wash their feet and say prayers with them before they were admitted. Their own clothing was often taken away to be cleaned and mended, and they were given hospital clothing to wear. People generally shared a bed – sometimes three people in a bed – although men and women were usually in separate dormitories.

Medieval hospital buildings tended to be tall and airy, with windows high up in the walls to let out "bad air". For heating, there was a fire in the centre of each dormitory, as well as small iron baskets filled with hot coals that could be moved around. Most hospitals had a separate kitchen where food was prepared and brought to the dormitories to be eaten twice a day.

Women in medicine

There were very few university-trained **physicians** in medieval times and, as we have seen, they came almost exclusively from noble or wealthy families. Women were excluded from their ranks, as they were not allowed to go to university, although there were a few women surgeons. Such doctors also treated only the upper classes of medieval society – nobles, wealthy merchants and townspeople, and important clerics. For most people, medical care started at home.

Everyday medical tasks for ordinary women in medieval times included getting rid of fleas or bedbugs (see the picture on the left) and headlice (right).

CAPVT. 118.

PUlex Ex li-
bro de na
turis rer.
Pulices
uocati
sūt, eo q
in pulue-
re magis
nutriunt.
Patet pu-
licem esse
uermicu
lū nigrū
& minu-
tum quidem, sed ualde pūgitiuum, maxi-
me autem tempore ęstiuo & pluuiali. Sali-
unt autem potius q uolāt, nocte q die ma
gis hominem infestant. Et nisi uehemens
torpor aut somnus grauis in membris sit,
se tueri non potest. Cum quis manum ad-

de cucumeris agrestis semina aqua reio-
luto sepe infuso.

CAPVT. 119.

PEdi-
cui9.
Isi. Pedi
culi sunt
uermes
cutis: à
pedibus
dicti: un
de pedi-
culosi di
cti suut,
qbus pe-
diculi in
corpore
efferues-
cunt. Ex libro de naturis rerum. Pediculi
dicuntur à numerositate pedum: hoc ma-
lum ex ipsa hominis carne creatur indubi
tanter, & tamen inuisibiliter, hos nonnul

WORD STATION
physician person qualified to practise medicine

HILDEGARDIS *a Virgin Prophetess, Abbess of St Ruperts Nunnerye. She died at Bingen A° Do: 1180 Aged 82 yeares.*

W.Marshall sculpsit.

HILDEGARD OF BINGEN
(1098–1179)

Hildegard was a noblewoman who was educated in a nunnery in medieval Germany and became a nun herself at the age of 15. From an early age, she had visions which she later wrote down in a series of religious texts. She was also an accomplished musician and herbalist, and wrote two medical texts. She became one of the most learned and respected women of her time.

Did you know?
Hildegard's medical works gave advice on practical matters such as hygiene, and the preparation of herbs and medicines.

Wise women

In most medieval towns and villages, it was women who carried out much of the everyday medical care. Many women knew enough about plants and herbs to make simple remedies for use in their homes. People also turned to local healers if they had a medical problem, often to "wise women". These were women who had knowledge of traditional medicine and remedies that had been passed down through generations.

Wise women were looked down on by educated physicians and distrusted by the Church, which suspected them of using magic. In fact, the treatments of wise women were mostly based on the belief that human life was in a delicate balance with the rest of nature. The theory of the doctrine of signatures (see page 16) reflected this. Wise women often gave people amulets that were worn to send away, and offer protection against, evil spirits. For example, necklaces made from the leaves of the angelica plant were believed to protect the wearer against illness, specifically the plague, and witchcraft.

Midwives

In the Middle Ages, babies were born at home. The birth was attended by a midwife and female relatives and friends. It was not considered acceptable for men to view a woman's "private parts", even in childbirth. For this reason, men were not allowed into the birthing room unless there was a problem, in which case a surgeon or a physician might attend. Many women learned midwifery by being apprenticed to more experienced midwives.

Midwives tried to help the mother by rubbing ointment on her stomach. When the baby was born, the midwife cut the umbilical cord and helped the child take its first breath. The baby was washed in warm water, or in milk or wine in wealthy households, then wrapped snugly in linen strips. This kept the baby warm and was also believed to help the limbs grow straight and strong.

This image from the 16th century shows a woman sitting on a special chair to give birth. The midwife works beneath her skirts to help deliver the baby.

TROTULA OF SALERNO
(1000s?)

Trotula was one of the few women in the medieval period who trained formally as a physician. Very little is known about her life, but it is thought that she attended and taught at the medical school in Salerno. She wrote many medical works about all aspects of women's health. She was the first to introduce the idea that both men and women may be responsible for **infertility** – a daring idea at that time. The illustration on the left is believed to be of her.

Did you know? Trotula advised the use of pain-numbing remedies to help women during childbirth. This was contrary to Christian teaching of the time that women should suffer the pain of childbirth as punishment for the sins of Eve in the Garden of Eden.

The end of the medieval period

We have seen that Europe became a wealthier place in the late Middle Ages, and that the practice of medicine became more organized and professional. For most people, however, these changes had little impact. Many continued to be treated by family members or local healers if they fell ill. There was no defence, for either rich or poor, against the ravages of illnesses such as the plague. Medical beliefs were still based on ideas that had come from the ancient Greeks and Romans. It was in the period that followed, the Renaissance, that these ideas began to be questioned, leading to major breakthroughs in medical science.

Timeline

AD	
476	The Western Roman Empire collapses
630s	Military expansion of the Islamic Empire across the Middle East, north Africa, and Asia begins
651	Hôtel-Dieu hospital is founded in Paris
c. 800s	**Monasteries** begin to develop as centres of medical care The first hospitals are established in Baghdad
c. 840	Hunayn ibn Ishaq (Johannitius) translates Greek and other medical books into Arabic
872	The first hospital is built in Cairo
c. 900s	*Leechbook* of Bald is written The medical school at Salerno, Italy is founded
c. 910	Al-Razi (Rhazes) identifies measles and smallpox, and writes many significant medical texts
c. late 900s	Abu al-Qasim (Albucasis) writes a surgical encyclopedia
c. 1000	Abdullah ibn-Sina (Avicenna) writes *The Canon of Medicine*
1000s	The practice of "king's touch" begins in England and France
c. 1000s	Trotula studies and teaches at Salerno
1088	The University of Bologna is founded
c. late 1000s	Constantine the African translates medical texts from Arabic into Latin
1100s	Thousands of leper houses are built in Europe The rise of universities across Europe occurs

1123	St Bartholomew's Hospital in London is founded
1163	The Catholic Church forbids the shedding of blood by monks
c. **1170**	The University of Paris is founded
1179	Hildegard of Bingen dies
1200s	Licensing of university-trained **physicians** begins
c. **1220**	The University of Montpellier is founded in France
1222	The University of Padua is founded in Italy
1247	The Priory of St Mary of Bethlehem (also known as the Bethlam Royal Hospital, or Bedlam) is founded in London
1268	The first recorded comment in the West (made by Roger Bacon) is made on the use of lenses in spectacle frames. However, lenses were probably used before this date in China.
1288	Santa Maria Nuova hospital is founded in Florence, Italy
1300s	The leprosy **epidemic** begins to die down
c. **1315**	The first public **dissection** takes place in Bologna, Italy
1347-1350	The Black Death devastates Europe
c. **1350**	Hospitals dedicated to healing the sick are developed

Glossary

anaesthetize give a patient a substance that produces loss of sensation, particularly of pain

anatomy bodily structure of a human, animal, or plant

apothecary person mainly in the medieval and Renaissance periods who prepared and dispensed medicines and remedies

aqueduct bridge or channel for moving water from one place to another

artery blood vessel that carries blood away from the heart

bile in medieval medical theory, two of the four humours are black and yellow bile. Bile is a bitter liquid produced by the liver, which helps the digestion of food.

bloodletting cutting veins to release blood

buboes swellings caused by inflamed glands in the body

cauterize in medieval and Renaissance medicine, a technique used to seal wounds by applying boiling oil or hot irons

cholera infection of the intestine that leads to diarrhoea and vomiting. It is most commonly transmitted through dirty drinking water or food.

convent religious community run by nuns

diagnose identify the nature of a disease or injury through examination

dissection process of cutting something up to learn about and understand its inner structure

dysentery disease transmitted through water or food that is contaminated by human excrement

epidemic rapid spread of a disease through an area or population

excrement waste matter from a human or animal body; faeces

hernia protrusion of an organ or tissue from its normal position, often caused by injury

humour in medieval medical theory, one of the four vital fluids thought to control the body

infertility inability to have babies

latrine toilet

microbe tiny organism that can carry disease

monastery religious community run by monks

patron saint protecting or guiding saint of a person, a group of people, or a place

pharmacologist someone who specializes in the preparation and study of drugs

pharmacy place where medicinal drugs are prepared or sold

phlegm mucus

physician person qualified to practise medicine

procedure surgical operation

public health prevention of disease and promotion of health through the organization of a community

quarantine keeping infected people in isolation in order to contain the spread of disease

repentance act of repenting a sin – that is, admitting wrong and trying to do better

scurvy disease caused by lack of vitamin C

unsanitary dirty and unhygienic

Find out more

Books

Medieval Realms: Death and Disease, Alex Woolf (Wayland, 2005)

Sci-Hi: Medical Technology, Ann Fullick (Raintree, 2011)

Sci-Hi: The Scientists Behind Medical Advances, Eve Hartman and Wendy Meshbesher (Raintree, 2011)

The History of Medicine: Medicine in the Middle Ages, Ian Dawson (Wayland, 2005)

When Disaster Struck: The Black Death 1347–1350, Cath Senker (Raintree, 2007)

Websites

www.sciencemuseum.org.uk/broughttolife
The Science Museum's History of Medicine website is divided into topics, including birth, diagnosis, and public health.

www.historyworld.net/about/wellcome.asp?gtrack=wtimeline
The Wellcome History of Medicine website includes information, timelines, and quizzes.

www.mostly-medieval.com
Explore this website to find out more about the medieval period. It contains a lot of information about medieval medicine, including an explanation of what different medicinal plants were used for.

www.godecookery.com/tacuin/tacuin.htm
Find out more about the *Tacuinum Sanitatis*.

www.bbc.co.uk/history/british/middle_ages/black_01.shtml
www.eyewitnesstohistory.com/plague.htm
Have a look at these websites to discover more about the Black Death.

Places to visit

This site provides a complete guide to the wide variety of medical museums in and around London.
www.medicalmuseums.org/home

Thackray Museum, Leeds
www.thackraymuseum.org

Museum of the Royal College of Surgeons, Edinburgh
www.museum.rcsed.ac.uk/content/content.aspx

Whipple Museum, Cambridge
www.hps.cam.ac.uk/whipple

More topics to research

- The effect the collapse of the Roman Empire had on medical knowledge in Europe

- Monasteries and convents in Europe

- The Order of Hospitallers founded in 1023 in Jerusalem to care for sick pilgrims

- Islamic hospitals in Baghdad, Cairo, and Damascus

- The aftermath of the Black Death

- The history of the Priory of St Mary of Bethlehem (also known as the Bethlam Royal Hospital, or Bedlam)

- The cover of this book shows a detail from a painting called *Cutting out the Stone of Madness or an Operation on the Head* by Pieter Bruegel the Elder. Find out more about the operation shown in the painting. What does it tell you about medical practices in the medieval period? Do you think cleanliness was as important in those days as it is today?

Index